My Family

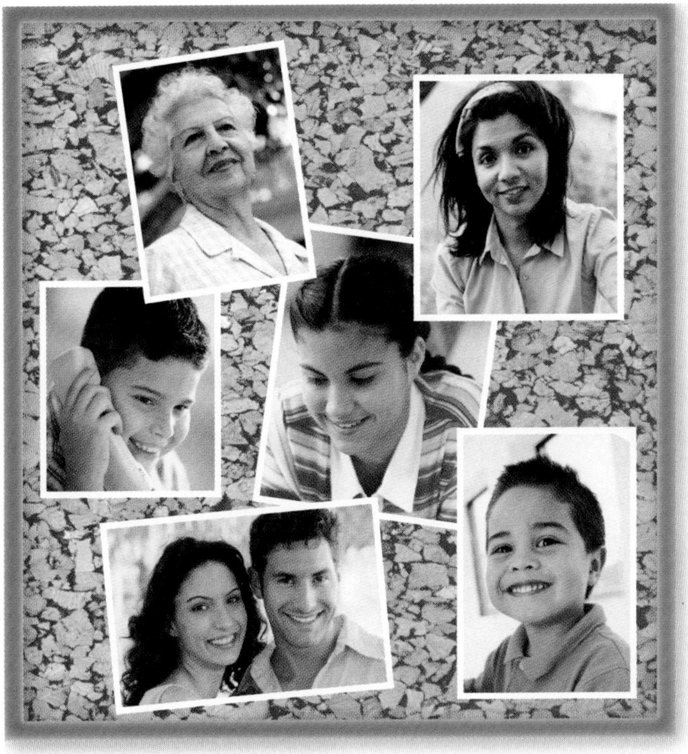

by Kathleen Theroux

HOUGHTON MIFFLIN BOSTON

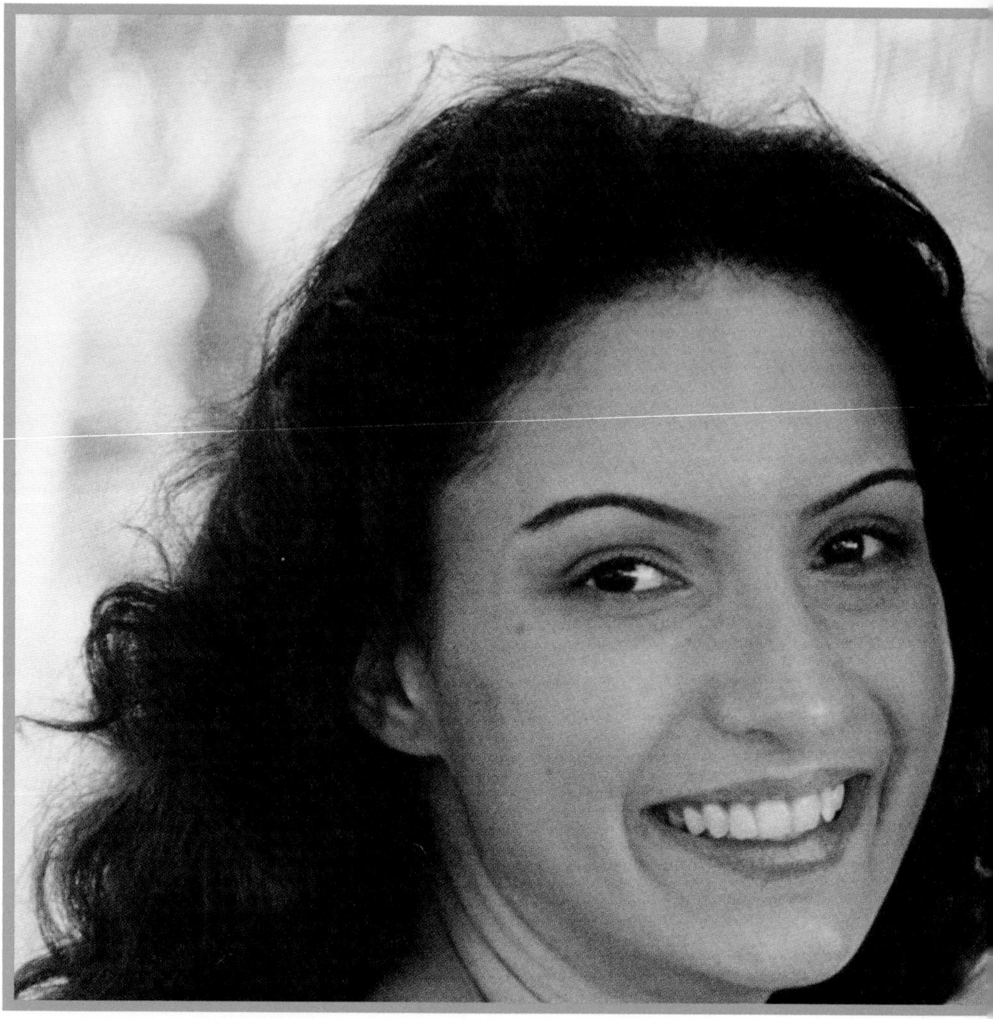

This is my mother.

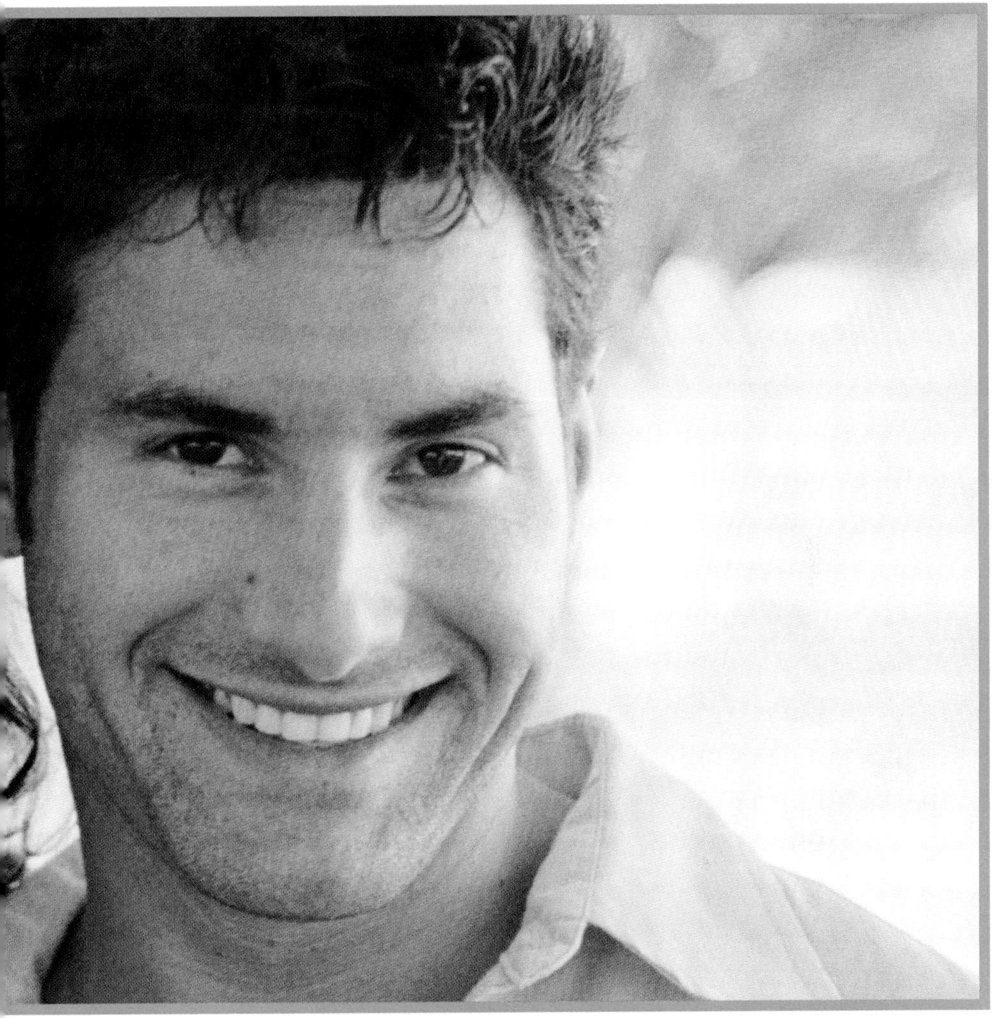

This is my father.

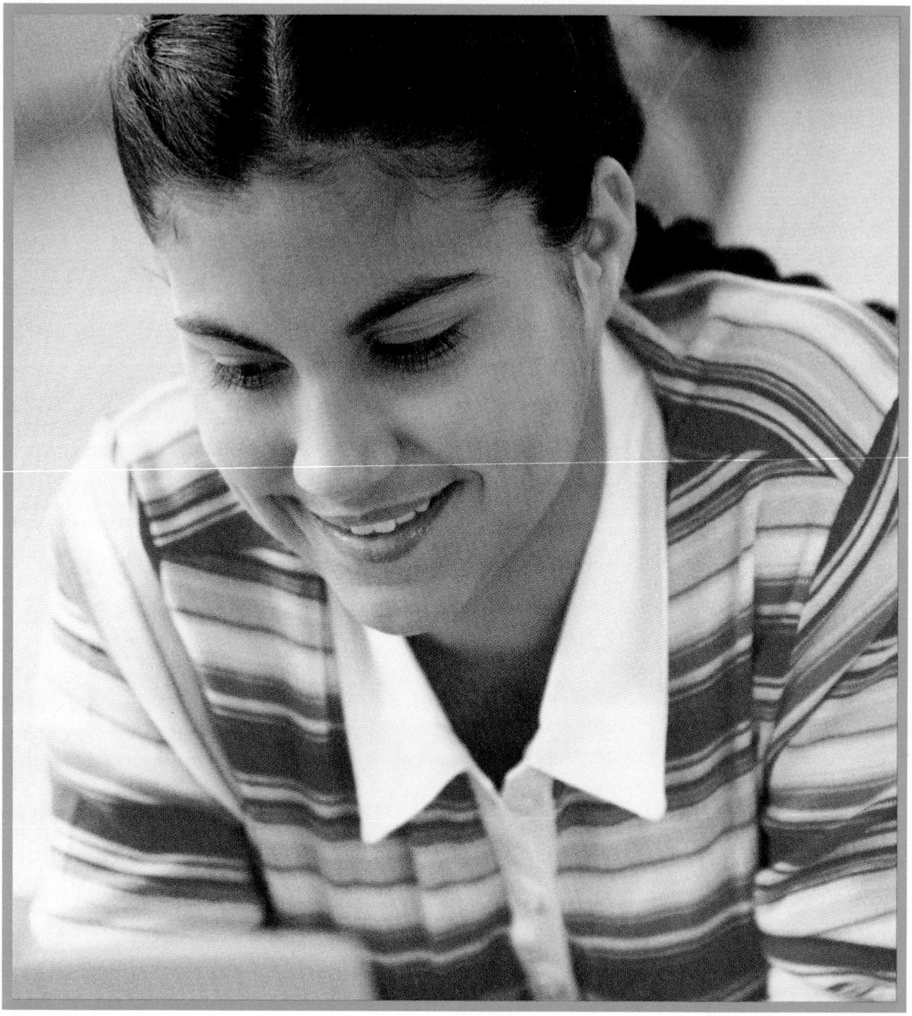

This is my sister.

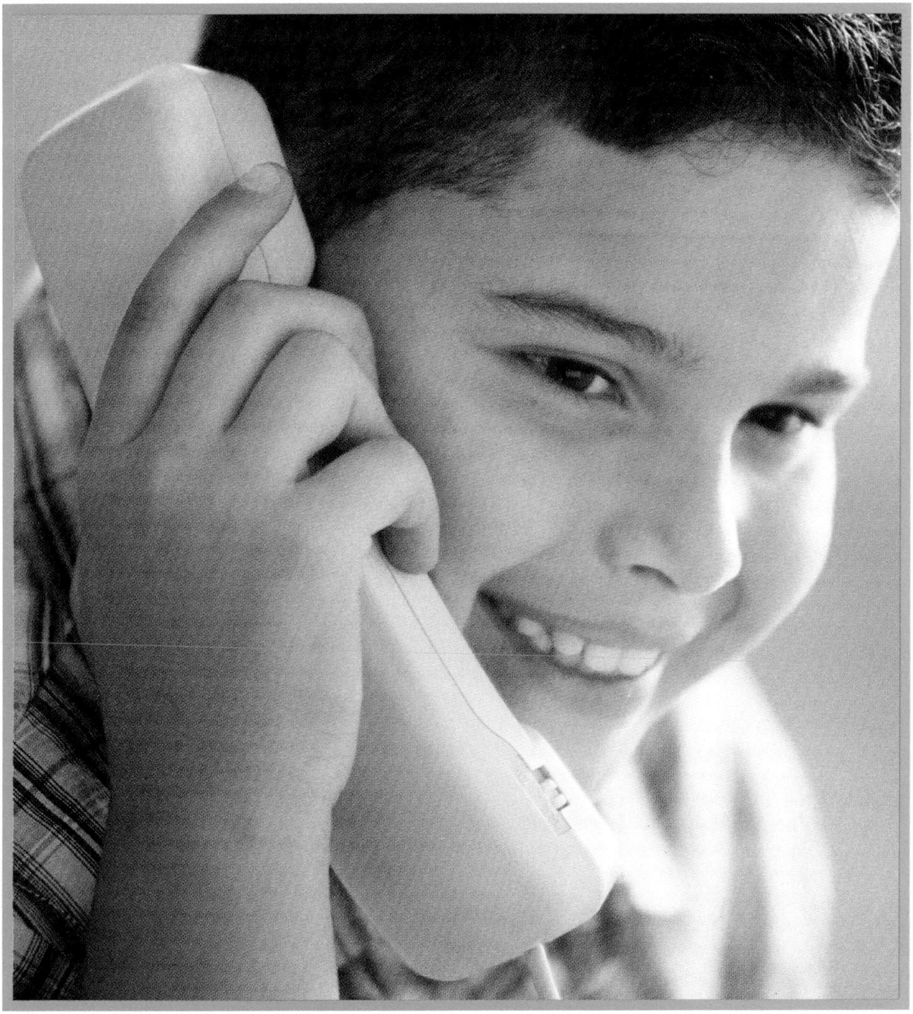

This is my brother.

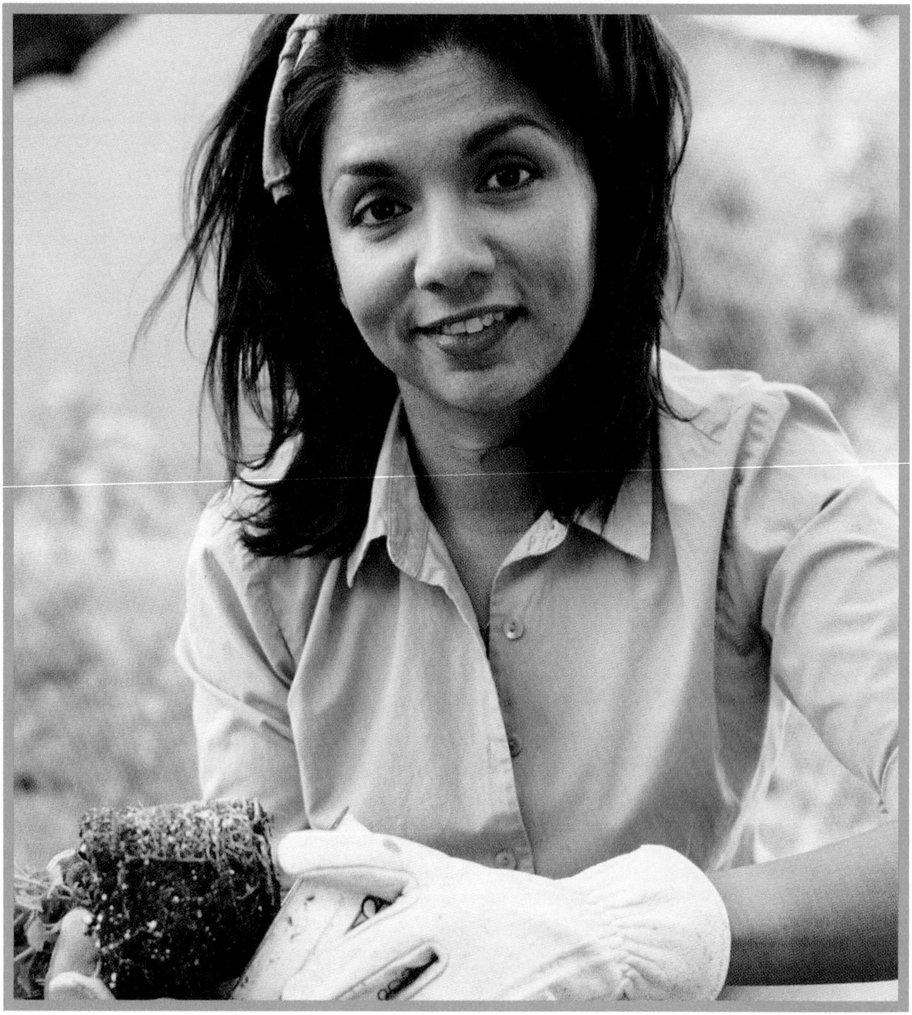

This is my aunt.

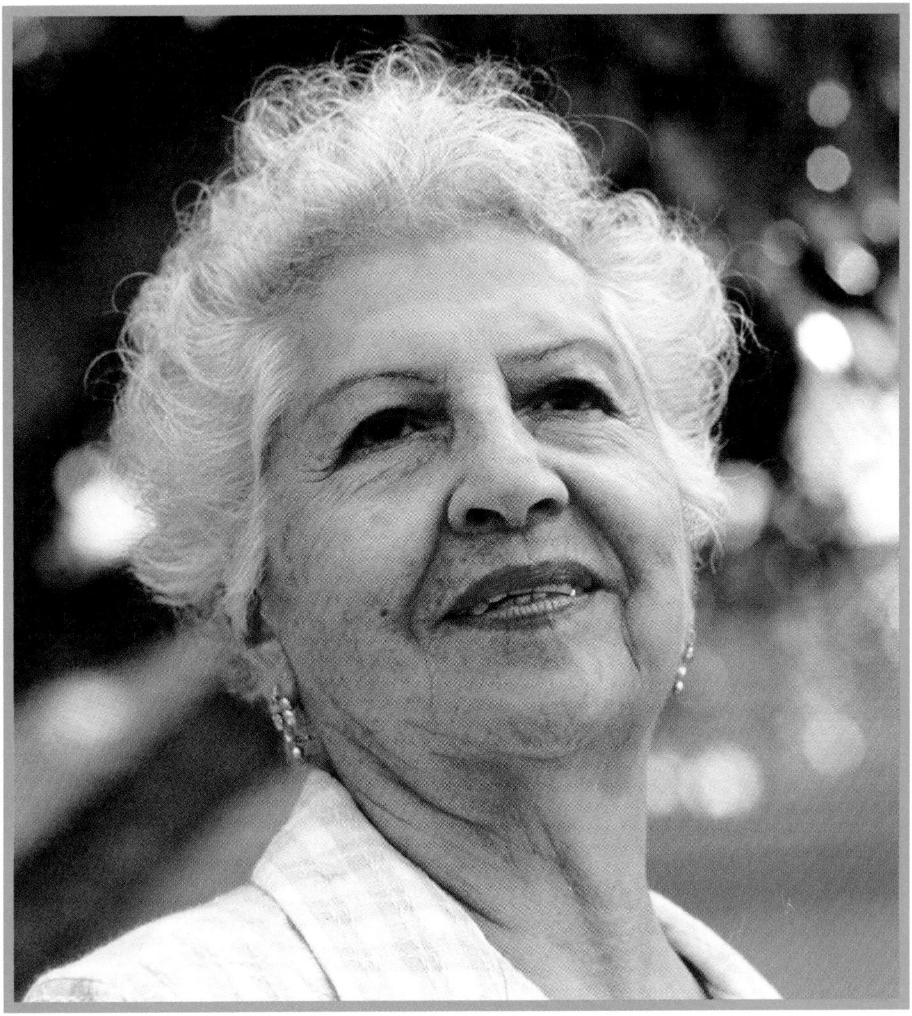

This is my grandmother.

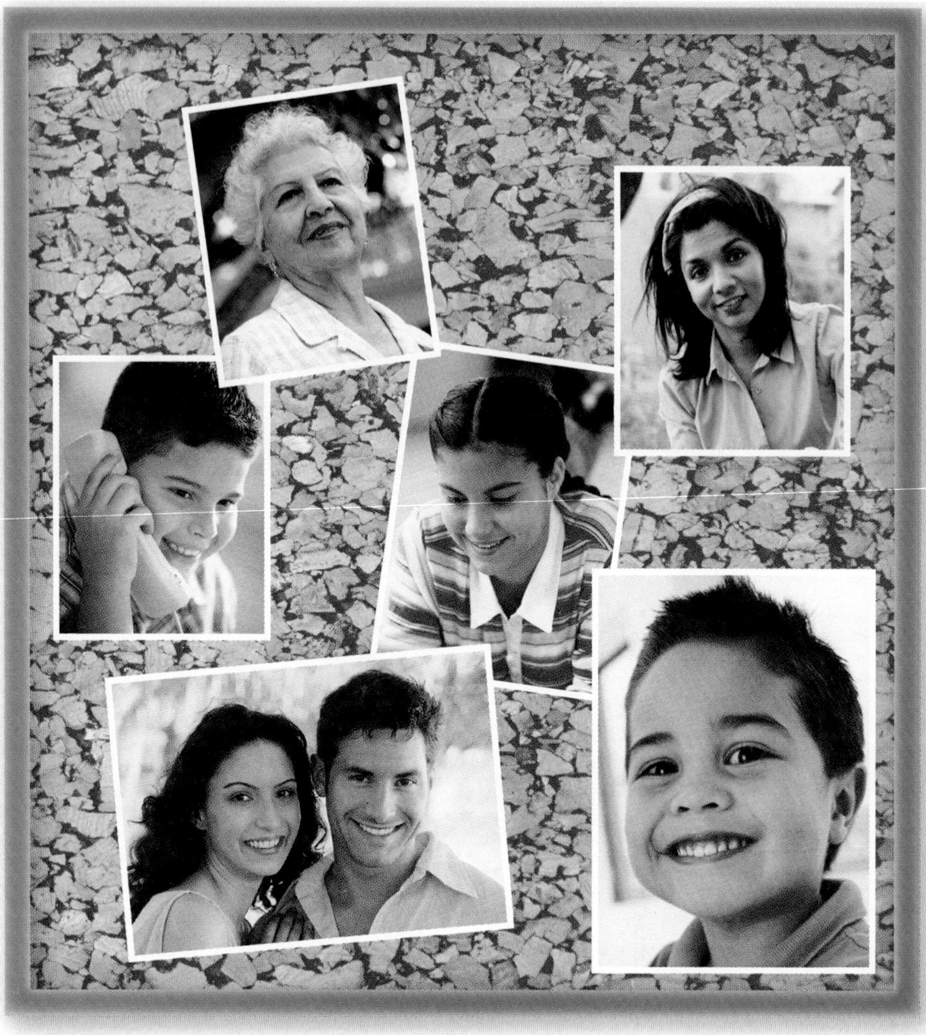

This is my family.